MINIMALISM 101

How Minimalist Living Can Help You To Declutter, Tidy Up Your Stuff and Say Goodbye to Things You Don't Need.

Kevin Garnett

© **Copyright 2020** by Kevin Garnett – All rights reserved.

In no way is it legal to reproduce, duplicate, or transmit any part of this document in either electronic means or in printed format. Recording of this publication is strictly prohibited and any storage of this document is not allowed unless with written permission from the publisher.

The information provided herein is stated to be truthful and consistent, in that any liability, in terms of inattention or otherwise, by any usage or abuse of any policies, processes, or directions contained within is the solitary and utter responsibility of the recipient reader. Under no circumstances will any legal responsibility or blame be held against the author for any reparation, damages, or monetary loss due to the information herein, either directly or indirectly.

The information herein is offered for informational purposes solely, and is universal as so. The presentation of the information is without contract or any type of guarantee assurance.

Medical Disclaimer: This book does not contain any medical advice. The ideas and suggestions contained in this book are not intended as a substitute for consulting with your doctor. All matters regarding your health require medical supervision.

Legal Disclaimer: all photos used in this book are licensed for commercial use or in the public domain.

ERRORS

Please contact me if you find any errors.

My publisher and I have taken every effort to ensure the quality and correctness of this book. However, after going over the book draft time and again, we sometimes don't see the forest for the trees anymore.

If you notice any errors, I would really appreciate it if you could contact me directly before taking any other action. This allows me to quickly fix it.

Errors: errors@semsoli.com

REVIEWS

Reviews and feedback help improve this book and the author.

If you enjoy this book, I would greatly appreciate it if you were able to take a few moments to share your opinion and post a review online.

Table of Contents

Introduction 7
PART 1: WHY MINIMALISM? 10
Chapter One: What Is Minimalism? 11
Chapter Two: Why Do We Accumulate So Much Stuff? 21
Chapter Three: The Benefits of Becoming A Minimalist 29
PART TWO: HOW TO BECOME A MINIMALIST 34
Chapter Four: First Steps for a Beginner Minimalist 35
Chapter Five: Where to Start as a Beginning Minimalist 47
Chapter Six: Things to Be Aware Of When Decluttering 57
Chapter Seven: Different Ways You Can Embrace Minimalism Every Day 65
PART THREE: HOW TO STAY A MINIMALIST 72
Chapter Eight: Tips on Sticking to Minimalism 73
Chapter Nine: What's Next? 79
Chapter Ten: The Mindset of a Minimalist (Your Minimalism Blueprint) 83
Final Words 87
Resources 89
BONUS CHAPTER: What is Stoicism 93
Did You Like This Book? 103

Introduction

I'm a minimalist. Or at least, I try to be.

What does this mean exactly? We'll look at what Minimalism is in Chapter One, but for now, it means that I live a simple life, one that is free from clutter, and one that is without stress.

I buy only what I need. I'm surrounded by objects that bring true value to my life. I see my friends and family regularly because that's what makes me content. I go cycling on Saturdays because I have free time to do that and it makes me feel good.

I live a life that is centered on simply the things I love doing and the things and people I value. I'm incredibly happy and have been ever since I started prioritizing my passions and discarding the things that don't add meaning to my life.

What's your secret, people ask me when they want to know why I'm so relaxed and at ease. The truth is, I don't have one. I just have a minimalist life. I focus on what brings me purpose and get rid of what doesn't.

It's a journey. It's not always easy, especially in the beginning, but it can be done with the right tools and know-how. And that's what this book, *'MINIMALISM 101: How Minimalist Living Can Help You To Declutter, Tidy Up Your Stuff and Say Goodbye to Things You Don't Need'* will teach you. I feel that now that I've achieved a minimalist life and it has brought me such fulfilment, it's my job to show others – which means: YOU – the way too.

In this book, you will find practical steps and action plans that will let you start a minimalist life right now. It will also guide you throughout your journey and show you how you can keep this lifestyle up.

So, without further ado, let's get started by learning what Minimalism is.

PART 1: WHY MINIMALISM?

Chapter One: What Is Minimalism?

In this chapter, we will define just what 'Minimalism' is and see just how widely-applied this concept is.

What is Minimalism

The term Minimalism applies when you reduce a subject to just its necessary elements and strip away the things that distract or don't add true value. It's a very much 'less is more' kind of concept.

Minimalism is used in art, music, literature, and architecture. In art, minimalist pieces are often based on geometric shapes, repetition, and neutral surfaces. In music, Minimalism takes shape in the iteration of simple sequences of chords. In literature, the written word is used sparingly, allowing the reader to engage with the text and draw out their own meaning of the work rather than see it through the author's eyes. In architecture, arguably one of the most well-known forms of Minimalism – thanks to the rise of the Japanese Zen philosophy in pop culture – is the style where a building or a room is minimized to the point where nothing more can be taken from the design to improve its look.

Seeing the pattern? Minimalism is all about letting the subject take the main stage by removing all the clutter and noise around it.

Minimalist Lifestyle

What is a minimalist lifestyle? It's when you get rid of your car, your house, live in an empty yet Zen-like white room, practice yoga every day, only eat wholesome organic food, travel to exotic yet peaceful destinations, and live with just a small suitcase of possessions.

I'm kidding! It's not like that at all.

However, some people are wary of a minimalist life as they feel it has all of these restrictions. They promptly decide that this is not for them as they couldn't possibly live without these things. Many people wrongly connect a minimalist lifestyle to a hippie way of living. They associate it to meditation and emptying your home of all its belongings. If that's what you want – to meditate, to clear your home out, to live as a hippie – that's great! If it makes you feel good and Minimalism can help you do that, of course.

However, if you think that Minimalism is just that, you're missing its real meaning.

Minimalism can be applied anywhere – from the financial broker, to the freelancer, to the stay-at-home mom or dad – and isn't just for those with loads of free time to enter a Zen-like state on a regular basis. In fact, you don't even need to give up everything you own. The real meaning of Minimalism is often distorted or exaggerated.

Minimalism doesn't frown upon having material possessions. It acknowledges that there isn't anything wrong in owning things. However, it also encourages you to think about how much value you assign to certain items. It invites you to minimize materialism, where we place so much significance on material goods that we prioritize it above other things in our life such as:

- friends and family,
- personal development
- pursuing passions
- our health, and
- contributions to society

It pushes you to think about what really matters and get rid of the stuff that doesn't.

If having a big house and a large garden is your dream and it matters to you, do it. Likewise, if traveling the world with just one suitcase is what makes you happy, then make it happen. Minimalism isn't about not spending or being extra frugal – it's about making conscious decisions about what items you want in your life that will bring value and help you achieve your goals. It's about thinking before you buy something impulsively that you don't need and can make you feel guilty after. It's about breaking out of the consumer culture, slowing down, and making purchases after careful deliberation. Minimalism helps align your values and goals with the items you have so everything around you serves a purpose, rather than being there for the sake of it.

People who follow a minimalist lifestyle don't all slot into one neat category. I follow a minimalist lifestyle and still have things such as a laptop and writing equipment. Naturally, I'm surrounded by friends and acquaintances, as we often are when we adopt a certain way of life or hobby, who also follow a minimalist lifestyle. My friend, Andrew Squires, travels regularly and can fit almost all his belongings into one large backpack, ready to embark on the next adventure. On the other hand, another friend of mine, Sofie Quinn, is excelling in her career in exports and has a house, a nice car, and still has a minimalist approach to life.

It's clear our lives are different yet we all share one common (and important) trait – we are all minimalists. How? Put simply, we have all surrounded ourselves with only the things we need or truly value by getting rid of the excess and clutter that were clouding out what really matters in our lives. We have deliberately chosen to seek out a life that is fulfilling and free, and one that is meaningful and full of purpose. Everything we have then contributes in some way to this, and ultimately to our happiness.

So, if I had to sum up Minimalism in one sentence, it would be:

Minimalism is the pursuit of happiness and fulfilment through life itself by following what drives us, rather than looking for purpose and meaning in material objects.

This is how Minimalism can be applied to anybody and everybody. Everyone has a different purpose in life and something that sparks their fire. Minimalism helps you find and nourish that, leading you to having a happier life that aligns your passions, your purpose, and your values.

It's not easy to adopt a minimalist lifestyle, at least not in the beginning. It requires deliberate thoughts and taking a long, hard look at what really matters to you. You need to be honest with yourself. However, it does get easier and eventually – I promise! – it becomes a mindset so ingrained that it's a part of you. Just keep taking it step by step and you will get there.

Everything in this book will help you, so don't worry about *how* to do it, as I will show you.

Action Steps

- Consider what you truly value and what is important to you. Is it having a family? Having a good job? Traveling? Buy a house? Perhaps it's all of these things.

- Take some time to deliberately think about what you value and make sure these are the things *you* want, not what you think others want for you.

- Make a list of what is important to you and what your goals are for the future. Make them as concise and detailed as possible. These may change in the future and that's fine. Right now, it's important to focus on how you are feeling and what drives you at this moment.

- These two lists are what give you your purpose. You want to be doing things that align with your values (what's important to you) and help you fulfil your purpose (your goals for the future).

- Keep these lists in an easy-to-see area so you are constantly reminded of who you are and where you want to be. This is the first step of beginning a minimalist life.

Chapter Two: Why Do We Accumulate So Much Stuff?

This chapter will look for answers to the big question – why do we accumulate so much stuff?

Undoubtedly, we are buying more things than ever before. A report by the Federal Reserve showed that the total amount of credit card debt in America exceeded $1 trillion in 2017! That's a huge amount of debt which clearly indicates that people are a) spending more than they have, and b) buying more products and goods than in the past.

These figures are alarming considering the repercussions that being in debt can have. It also suggests a steady change in values in society where goods and materials are becoming increasingly important for our perceived well-being. But are they really doing us any good?

The truth is, we tend to buy more than we need. Almost all of us have
experienced a time when we:

- bought clothes we didn't need (or never used)
- cooked food that ended up being thrown away, or
- bought games for kids that get left in a corner after five minutes of play.

This over-consumption can lead to debt, depression (if you can't pay your debts, it can lead to stress and despair), and feelings of guilt.

So, why do we do this to ourselves? Why do we amass so many things that, truthfully, we don't really need?

There are actually several reasons why and they tend to be more complex and unconscious than we realize. They also interact; our impulses to buy are often a combination of different motives.

Security

Buying lots of things can make us feel secure. We may not consciously realize this, but buying more materials makes us feel safe, such as a house, a car, clothing, plenty of food, etc. Think of it as having a nest where we constantly add more and more things to give that sense of security. Many of us think having a house and car ticks off the major things we need in life to feel established. Our brains automatically make the assumption that owning more and more will give us even more safety. It's not just security in terms of our well-being; it can also link to security relating to our perceived position in society.

Advertising and Influencers

The vast majority of us like to think we are too clever for an advert to convince us to buy something and that we make consumer choices based on our own free will. The truth is (and it's a hard one to deliver and to take!) that we are far more influenced by advertising than we like to believe.

Social media is extraordinarily apt at delivering marketing messages that are tailored to our individual needs and the growth of influencers on Instagram, Facebook, and other online platforms strongly shape our purchases. On average, we see between 300 and 700 marketing messages a day that try, whether it's obviously or subtly, to convince us that buying their product will somehow make our lives better. Marketing is a science and a fascinating one, so I'm not by any means having a dig at advertising; rather, I'm pointing out a factor that can guide us to purchase more.

Jealousy

This is a case of 'keeping up with the Joneses'. We see what other people have and we compare that to what we have. If all of our friends have it, then it's more likely that we will want to buy it too. This can lead us to buying more technology than we truly need, more clothes than we truly need, and purchasing things that we can't really afford.

Happiness

Buying makes us happy – or at least, that's what we think it does. Many people look for happiness in purchases. However, the truth is: that feeling of euphoria that we get when we buy something new is just a temporary state. It doesn't last, nor does it accumulate. It usually doesn't add to our personal development or goals, and the positive feelings we have are short-lived. Most of us have experienced a moment when we *have* to buy that new coat or we *must* get the newest mobile phone. The impulse is so strong that it often makes us buy in excess.

For example, Lucia Santos, an acquaintance of mine who is just beginning her journey as a minimalist, went on a large shopping splurge recently and when I asked her why, she replied, *"I felt like buying new clothes, I needed them."* I asked her to look a bit deeper and she was adamant that she truly had nothing to wear and has to get new clothes. When we talked about what had she been doing before, she revealed that she had been just been doing housework and in between chores, looking at Instagram. *"It was then it clicked"*, she said. *"I follow a lot of lifestyle and fashion accounts and when I see those immaculately-dressed models, my own wardrobe feels just so frumpy. I wanted clothes like the models have so I went out and bought so many new things."* Does she feel different now? *"Not really. I mean, I like most of my new clothes but I still feel inadequate to those Instagram pages and I kind of regret spending so much money."*

This is a common scenario and probably all of us know it very well. This example serves to show that you need to dig deep to discover what is motivating you to buy in excess.

Buy To Impress

We rarely, if ever, admit we are buying more things than we need to impress others. It doesn't sound very cool when you say it out loud, does it? Yet it is true and we are pretty much all susceptible to this, especially if you are growing up in a wealthy or well-developed society where the consumer economy depends on us buying more and more, to show off our success and status in the world. It's one of the hardest motives to admit, yet peer pressure is powerful.

Action Steps

- Think about your last shopping splurge. What drove you to it? What happened before you went on a huge shopping spree? We are trying to discover what was the motive for you to buy in excess or buy things you perhaps didn't need. It can be so subtle that you can't identify it in the beginning. Keep looking hard and you will find it.

- Try pinpointing the reasons why you buy things – is it necessity or something else? – to help you become more aware and conscious about your purchases.

Chapter Three: The Benefits of Becoming A Minimalist

This chapter will explore the benefits of becoming a minimalist and living a lifestyle without an excess of material possessions. There are many positive effects that Minimalism can bring you.

Freedom

Excessive amounts of material items accumulate until we amass a pile of stuff that we don't need and ends up anchoring us down. It traps us in a state of fear as well, as we become emotionally tied to our belongings and scared of losing things. If we whittle down our possessions to just the things we truly need, we also end up letting go of many negative things in our life such as debt, obsession, misplaced values (for example, valuing materials more than your health), and greed.

Happiness

Ironically, we tend to think that the more we buy, the happier we'll be – when in fact the opposite is true; the less we have in terms of material possessions, the happier we tend to be. As long as we are aware of our purpose, values, and goals. Getting rid of the clutter helps us see that there isn't as much meaning in materials as we often think there is and makes it easier to find out what our priorities really are.

Different Perspectives

We tend to focus a lot on material items, which gives them a much higher perceived importance than they often deserve. Like I mentioned before, there is nothing wrong about having things; the problem is when we start buying things we don't need, just because we think they will bring us happiness or fill some sort of void. A minimalist lifestyle allows us to adjust our priorities and concentrate on what really brings value to our lives.

Focus on What is Important

If you declutter and get rid of everything that doesn't help you fulfill your true goals and purpose, you are only surrounded by stuff that adds value to your life. This helps you create an environment that directly connects to your 'bigger picture' and helps you accomplish the things you want. The old expression that talks about surrounding yourself with good people, and people who you aspire to be like, can definitely be applied to possessions too. Weed out the stuff you don't need and focus on what's important instead.

Save Money

A minimalistic lifestyle means you only buy things that you need, or that speed up your personal growth. If you stop buying in excess, you will save money. This can help you accomplish your dreams, such as traveling more, or doing courses, to get you on the career path you want.

Environmentally Friendly

Buying less stuff means you are one less person contributing to the excessive production and waste of plastic and other harmful by-products of consumption.

Action Steps

- One of the action steps in Chapter One was creating a list of values and goals that are important to you. Take a look at this list again and see which of the above benefits are the best fit for your values.

- For example, if contributing to society is something that is extremely important to you, the advantage of being environmentally friendly with a minimalist lifestyle helps support your values. If family and friends are your priority, then being happier from a minimalist lifestyle means you can be a joy in your loved ones' lives. If your career is your focus, then the purpose and drive a minimalist lifestyle brings will help you achieve your goals.

- By linking the advantages to your values and goals, you can see how the minimalist lifestyle is good for you. It will strengthen your willpower to keep on pursuing a life free from clutter. Use this when you feel you need some extra support.

PART TWO: HOW TO BECOME A MINIMALIST

Chapter Four: First Steps for a Beginner Minimalist

This chapter will look at how to begin the journey of a minimalist lifestyle.

Where to Start

So, you've decided Minimalism is for you and now you want to start. The question is, where do you begin? The good news: you've *already* started! The lists of your values and purchase-trigger points from Part One will have already helped you align yourself closer to your values, goals and priorities and made you consciously aware of how your actions, and what surrounds you, will influence them. Keep this at the forefront of your mind, as this will help you over the course of the next chapters.

The next step, and what this chapter is all about, is to create a minimalist environment. This means taking a good, long look at your home and reducing your stuff to what you need, rather than what you keep simply for the sake of keeping. A bonus point with this step is that a minimalist home can look incredibly beautiful from a design point of view. So, not only will this activity help you to declutter your life, it will actually make your home look even better.

One thing worth mentioning before we continue is this: creating a minimalist environment is all about having a stress-free life and creating more meaning. So, don't obsess over how many items you have or don't have. Don't worry if you feel there are some things you just can't throw away. The point is, you are trying to simplify your life. If you take it step-by-step, you will get there. It gets easier and at the end of the day, this is your personal journey to have a meaningful life. You are just at the beginning, so enjoy it and let your minimalist side develop naturally without being too hard on yourself.

Now, before we look at how to declutter your home and create this minimalist environment that we've talked about, it's important to recognize the difference between what you need and what is good.

What do I mean by that?

The problem many of us have is that we can't throw something out simply because it is a good product, or in good condition, or it's a good brand. We keep it because of its quality or perceived attributes rather than if we need it or not. This is one of the key concepts you need to learn before decluttering your home.

Need Vs Good

Let's imagine you have a multi-purpose pot in your kitchen that functions perfectly well as a pressure cooker as well as many other appliances. Let's say you also have a separate pressure cooker at home which you never use as the multi-purpose pot does the job fine. The problem is, this pressure cooker is a great brand and brand new, so you definitely don't want to get rid of it. It cost a lot of money and maybe you'll need it one day! How do you solve this dilemma?

First of all, recognize that just because something is 'good' in some way, doesn't mean that you actually need it. This is important to know, as it's one of the main reasons we tend to hold onto things; we give them meaning because of its perceived quality, rather than it being something that is adding value to our lives.

This pressure cooker may be the best in the business. However, you never use it and you already have something that works just as well. As you have a perfectly good substitute, you won't even notice that it's not there when it's gone; it's just that, right now as you're looking at it, you are reminded of its 'goodness'.

What about keeping it for future use? This is a slippery slope to go down as in theory, we could potentially keep everything based on this logic. The thing is, right now you don't need it and your multi-purpose pot works just fine. Even if it breaks one day, it's more probable that you will just buy another one, given its effectiveness and your familiarity with it. So, the other pressure cooker will just end up sitting there and never be used.

How about the fact that it cost a lot of money? When I say 'get rid of things', I don't necessarily mean throw it away. There are other ways to remove things out of your life. When Anna, a friend of mine who is trying out the minimalist lifestyle, decided to declutter her home, there were a lot of things she didn't want to throw away. *"I love to cook"*, she said. *"And I have loads of kitchen utensils and cooking equipment, more than I even cared to think about. When I started clearing out my kitchen, I found so many duplicate items and it was making my kitchen chaotic. The problem was, they were expensive and I had a hard time thinking about just throwing them out."*

It's a familiar story. We feel like we somehow lose money when we simply chuck things away. However, Anna revealed her solution: *"Many of my items were new and never used so I sold what I could on local Facebook groups as it meant I didn't even need to post the items. People could come and pick them up or we could meet nearby. I didn't make all of my money back of course but just having something in return felt nice."*

What about the items she couldn't sell? *"I donated them to charity or gave them to friends and family who liked them,"* she said. *"Giving stuff away actually felt just as good as selling it and it helped me feel like I'd done a good deed."*

How To Categorize Your Items

It's tricky to decide what to do with your items, and harder still breaking the ties we attach to our material possessions. When you're sorting through your things, try to decide which of the five following categories they belong to:

- Sell
- Recycle
- Donate
- Keep (because you need them), and
- Discard

Doing this gives you a sense of direction when organizing through your belongings. The well-known rule is that if you haven't used it for more than 6 months, it has to go. We probably all have an item of clothing somewhere that we hold onto because 'one day we will use it' yet we never do. It's things like this that we have to overcome and get rid of.

Anna sold or donated her unwanted items. Donating is such a fantastic thing to do, as it really helps people who have items that they genuinely need but are not in a position to buy. Clothes and books in particular are great to donate. You can leave them at charity shops or at homeless shelters. Alternatively, if you have loads of items, you could have a jumble sale and use the earnings to donate to a charity of your choice. By having a higher purpose in mind when decluttering, it can really help you to be more determined with what you keep and what you get rid of.

You can also recycle, which is especially good for old books with pen marks, used notebooks, or glass items. It will help you feel that you are doing your bit for the world as a whole and you genuinely will be doing something useful and positive.

Sentimental Items

Sentimental items are one of the hardest things to approach when you are decluttering your home. However, there are some ways of making it easier.

Note: remember that being a minimalist is keeping things you value and relate to your purpose rather than literally getting rid of everything. If sentimental items are important to you due to their connections to loved ones, then by all means, keep them and don't feel you need to throw them away. The suggestions below are simply if you feel you want to get rid of the sentimental items but are unsure how to do it in a sensitive way.

Things like old letters and photos are hard to let go of and if they belong to passed loved ones, it's not necessarily something you would ever dream of throwing out – and that's fine. If they bring value to you and you like to flick through them regularly, then having these memories close at hand can bring comfort and fit with values surrounding family. If on the other hand you haven't looked at these old keepsakes for years, why not consider passing it along to another family member who may want to look through them? It might bring them immense joy seeing past family memories in the flesh so to speak and if the time comes when they stop revisiting these items regularly, they can pass them onto another family member to keep the memories alive.

If you have old childhood toys that you love but haven't seen the light of day for years after being left in the attic, why not donate them to younger members of your family? They may love these older, classic toys and this way your precious possessions still remain in the family. You could take photos of them before if you like so at least you will have some memory of them.

One Room at a Time

Begin in one room and make your way through your apartment or house. I like to start at my desk as that's the place that gets cluttered the most – old magazines, notes, leaflets, that kind of thing. All paper goes to recycle, and magazines that I've already read or had for a while either get recycled or donated. Start at the place where you feel most motivated to begin and build up momentum from there. Remember to really think about whether you need the item or not. Be as honest as you can be to yourself.

You may find you need to do little bits over the course of a few days and that's totally fine. Do it at your own pace; the most important thing is to just go ahead and do it.

Here is one of my top tips for you: after minimizing your entire home, the sense of satisfaction is immense and you will feel so good. I like to use this feeling to motivate me to take another sweep around the house and see if there is anything else I can discard. Once I let go of so many things, I feel lighter and freer, which gives me confidence to let go of even more material possessions. So, once you've decluttered for the first time, try going in for a round two of decluttering. You may be surprised by how much more you can strip away!

Action Steps

- Start in a place where you have a lot of clutter. This is usually a place such as a desk, a wardrobe, or an attic (this is probably the most cluttered place in the house!) and begin to organize everything.

- Assess each item by whether you need it or not. Be as honest as possible.

- To help you, categorize each item – keep, discard, sell, donate, recycle. This will help you approach your decluttering with a logical mind.

- Take your time. It may be a big job to declutter everything so it's totally fine to do it a bit at a time. Focus on how you feel after you declutter a particular area. The sense of lightness is you cutting ties with material possessions and taking another step towards a more meaningful life.

Chapter Five: Where to Start as a Beginning Minimalist

This chapter looks at some of the most important points and practical steps you can take when starting your journey as a minimalist.

If you're new to Minimalism, then it's worth reading and ingraining in your mind the following points. It will help you simplify things from the start and guide you towards a happier and healthier life. Bear in mind that this isn't the one and only path to a simpler and more meaningful life, but it's a good one nonetheless and can help you achieve a minimalist lifestyle.

Why Do You Want to Live a Minimalist Lifestyle?

First of all, understand why you want to live a minimalist lifestyle.

This is important to know as it will be the core of your motivation and the reason that drives you. What is your motive? Why do you want to simplify your lifestyle? For me, I wanted to live in a stress-free environment and focus on my personal development and professional goals. I found that with less distractions in my life, I could do this better. Yours could be totally different. Maybe you want to focus on your family or your health, perhaps you want to feel free or travel to new destinations. Whatever it is you want, make a note of it and expand each point with how Minimalism will allow you to achieve this. This will help you understand your motive better and build a tie to it. Once that is clear, everything else begins to fall into place.

Build a Network

Next, build a network. Don't do this alone.

The thing that helped me the most when I embarked on a minimalist lifestyle was the fact that I was surrounded by people that were already living minimally or people that were interested in the concept. Of course, not all my friends and family are interested and that's fine. Some support me more than others and that's fine too. We can't all like and appreciate the same thing. However, I'm lucky that I have some close friends who are minimalists and have introduced me to others who think the same way.

What should you do then if no one you know is in the same, minimalist mindset as you want to be? You can still immerse yourself in a minimalist way of thinking by listening to podcasts and reading books and blogs on Minimalism. One of the most popular and common ways of meeting other people in an area that is outside your regular social circle is by using social media. Search on Facebook to find dozens of groups about

Minimalism. Engaging in these groups and chatting to people there – even if it is online – can really help you feel connected to others and supported by like-minded people.

Start with Baby Steps

Take your time to embrace a minimalist lifestyle by starting with baby steps.

Take each day one at a time and make small steps towards Minimalism. Minimalism isn't just about cleaning your house out; it's about adopting a new lifestyle. It takes time for your mindset to fully adapt to this new approach. Decluttering your home is a great start – but it's not the only thing to do. Once you free your environment of unnecessary material items, you need to be able to not rush out and buy more things and be comfortable using only what you need. This takes time to get used to and you should do it slowly. Also, don't feel guilty if the journey isn't perfect and you slip up. It's normal and nothing is perfect. What's important is you get back up and continue forward.

Preparation

One of those baby steps is preparation.

Knowing what to expect, and preparing yourself to deal with the challenges and changes ahead, can put you in a good position to keep progressing. At some point, you may look into your wardrobe and the minimal amount of clothes may trouble you. Or you look at your bare table and it makes you feel uneasy and you want to buy more things to add to your surfaces, your shelves, or your drawers. This happens because we have been conditioned for so long that consumer culture is the norm and that 'retail therapy' is a cure. Be prepared for these feelings. When they come, use it as an opportunity to think about what matters to you and embrace that. If it's your health, instead of going out to buy things, go for a run to clear your head. If it's your family, instead of concerning yourself with empty drawers, call your relatives or arrange to spend time with a friend, if that's what truly makes you happy. Do the things that make you feel good and the things you love doing in your spare time. This will help those unpleasant feelings go.

Make it Fun

Remember though, simplifying and living a minimalist lifestyle isn't all serious and strict. Make it fun.

One of the main reasons and positive outcomes of a minimalist lifestyle is that it gives you the time and freedom to concentrate on the things that you truly want from your life and to do the things you love. You can't get more fun than that! So, keep that in mind. You're trading material possessions to exercise, to be with your children, to go out with your friends, to travel, to develop, to move up in your career, or whatever reason you have to be a minimalist. Secondly, having less clothes, for example, will encourage you to actually use them all and experiment with different styles. Just search online to see how many different ways you can use a plain white t-shirt to see the potential you have to vary your style and add a bit of playful flair to your attire.

Take Time Out

Minimalism is more than just getting rid of material possessions; it's about simplifying everything and giving yourself time to enjoy the things you love. Take at least 15 minutes from your day to look out of the window and enjoy the view, to sit in the park and take in the surroundings, to get lost in your own thoughts in a quaint café, to stretch and meditate, to do anything that gives you time to connect with your thoughts and just simply be. It can be strange at first not having anything to do other than appreciate what's going on around you, but try to relax and feel the stress go.

Start Now

It's worth remembering that you don't need to wait to start living a life centered on your goals and passions. You can start *now*.

Minimalism helps you make deliberate choices about what you do with your time and how you spend your efforts and energy. The great thing about it is that you don't need to wait until you have emptied your wardrobe or decluttered your car or paid off your credit card or until you have a concise list of all your values. You can start right now by simply taking a little bit of your day to relax or pursue a passion. Start instantly to take the first step and let it evolve from there.

Be Kind to Yourself

This Minimalism journey is all about taking it slow and simplifying your life. Charging at this new lifestyle at 100 miles per hour won't help you stick to it. Take it slow, enjoy it, and do it at your own pace and definition. Just because someone can put all of their life belongings in one suitcase does not make you any less of a minimalist. You don't even need to call yourself that. Just do what you can to make your life simpler in your own personal way.

Action Steps

- Get a pen and some paper and decide exactly what it is that has drawn you to the minimalist way of life. Write down what you hope to achieve and how Minimalism could help you with that. Making these connections will help make things clearer.

- Take out 15 minutes of your day where you can be by yourself. Use this time not to plan what you will do tomorrow or to think about a work meeting, but to empty your thoughts and just *be*. Think about your passions or read a book. Just spend this time in the moment and shut everything off. This is important to help you reconnect to your environment, slow down, and destress; in other words, to make things simple.

Chapter Six: Things to Be Aware Of When Decluttering

This chapter looks at important things to be aware of when decluttering. Think back to Chapter Four when we talked about how to minimalize your home and reduce the amount of material possessions. You can reach a point where decluttering itself becomes a new obsession and may not be leading you along the path you want to be on. This chapter addresses that and will guide you to get back on track should you need it.

Decluttering is an important part of the minimalist lifestyle. It helps us to simplify things and to focus on what we truly want. It's a great starting point for embarking into Minimalism. However, you can reach a point where decluttering can actually make you lose sight of the real point of Minimalism. You can end up not feeling good if you can't discard of enough things or are unable to simplify as quickly as you want. When this happens, you may just need to refocus your attention onto something else, such as your passions or our goals. As I said, decluttering is great and powerful; but it's not the be-all and end-all of Minimalism. Do it once and it's merely being organized; you have to adopt Minimalism as a *lifestyle*.

So, here are some things to be aware of that will help you to think about if you are decluttering too much and to guide you back onto the Minimalism path. If you find yourself doing any of the following while trying to adopt the minimalist lifestyle, it's better to go back to looking at what your motives are for starting this journey in the first place and try to realign yourself and your actions with that.

You're Decluttering – And Then Going Out and Shopping

Sometimes we will end up buying something we don't need. If that happens, we should simply identify the trigger, to help us learn to deal with that urge differently next time. This is normal; it's all a part of the journey.

The problem occurs when, after you have decluttered your home, you find yourself searching online for new clothes or wandering around the department store filling your trolley with new ornaments and things to decorate your home with. In this case, you have decluttered simply to provide more space to buy more things. Try taking it slowly and spend some time in your decluttered space. Sometimes, that feeling of a room with few things in it sparks that desire to consume and we need to spend time adjusting to this new environment. Slow down with your decluttering by doing it bit by bit, so you have time to adapt. It can be a shock to go from having so much to much less, so ease yourself into it.

You're Decluttering – But Feeling Bad Because Of It

It's not easy to declutter, which is why I mentioned some tips to decluttering your home in Chapter Four. However, if you are really struggling to get rid of things, and it's making you feel bad or angry or upset that you can't let go and don't want to let go, then slow down. Take a break. Remember, small steps are fine. You don't have to go from having way more than you need to just having the basic essentials. It's all about slowly discarding things. If you can even remove some things in the beginning, that is a great start, as long as you feel good about it. If you feel negative at any point, stop and rethink your values. Stop decluttering for a while. Talk to your support network about this, whether that's your friends, family, or online support groups.

You're Decluttering – But Feel Like You're in a Rush to Finish It

Decluttering and simplifying your life is a process and ideally, a lifelong one at that. It's not a chore to add to your to-do list, nor is it something you must do as quickly as possible. If you find yourself rushing to complete your task – to declutter your home as quickly as possible or comparing your simplifying efforts to those of others – you are not on the right track. Your intentions may be well-meaning, but in this state, you won't be able to keep up a long-term change or achieve the happiness that Minimalism can bring.

Take a step back and appreciate that Minimalism isn't a race and there is no end point; it is, in fact, a series of small steps to simplify your life and remove stress. It requires continuous efforts and consciousness. Slow down and stop comparing yourself to others. Only resume with your decluttering when you are ready to recognize it as your own personal journey.

Action Steps

- If you are currently in the process of decluttering, take a step back and stop for a minute. Relax and ask yourself the following questions – Are you feeling bad? Do you feel like you are in a race to get everything done? Is this just another chore on your list? Are you mentally noting what new things you need to buy, as you are throwing out the old?

- If you answered 'yes' to any of the above, stop what you're doing and take another look at your values. Remind yourself why you are doing this. Then do something else other than decluttering. It doesn't matter how long it takes you – remember, this is not a race and you haven't failed – just make sure you start again when you truly feel this is a part of your personal journey.

- If you answered 'no' to the above questions, then carry on doing what you are doing. And I can't stress this enough – whether you answer 'yes' or 'no', it doesn't matter and no one is better or worse, or right or wrong. Everyone is different and sometimes we have obstacles to overcome that are a result of our own unique experiences that can make some things easier for some, harder for others.

Chapter Seven: Different Ways You Can Embrace Minimalism Every Day

This chapter will look at simple ways in which you can embrace Minimalism every day, no matter where you are or what you are doing.

The great thing about being a minimalist is there is no right or wrong way of doing it. You can start small, such as having a minimalist approach to your:

- Interior design
- Clothes
- Makeup, or
- Traveling in the simplest means possible.

You can apply it to just one area of your life or you can embrace Minimalism in every aspect of your day.

Shopping

Just because you are a minimalist, that doesn't mean you can't go shopping anymore. Not at all – we all genuinely need new things sometimes. Rather than giving up shopping all together and bracing yourself for the next year of using the same clothes, towels, and bed linen until they go to dust, Minimalism encourages you to be conscious when you are shopping and make careful, deliberate choices. When you go to the supermarket, take a list with you of everything you need and just buy those items. I know it's often all too tempting when you see a promotion that is *such* a bargain that it would be a crime to leave it, but this is the consumer culture at work again. Stick to your list and when you get home, you probably will have forgotten that amazing promotion anyway.

Start Saying 'No'

Minimalism isn't all about having a material-free place. It's about you leading the life you want without distractions. One of the most important things we could all learn is how to say 'no' to things we don't want to do. It's all too easy to say yes to your boss when he asks you to work overtime when you don't want to, or to agree to go out for dinner with your friends when you're tired and just want to stay at home, especially if you are a people-pleaser. One of the main reasons we do this is because we are worried how the other person will react – maybe they will be upset, offended or even get angry. However, the reality is they probably won't mind at all and at the end of the day, you are not responsible for how they react to your 'no'. Next time someone asks you to go out with them and you don't want to, try saying 'no' and concentrate on doing what you truly want to do.

Experiences, Not Things

Start making this your mantra if it helps – experiences over things. Rather than buying material items, think of the experiences you could have instead and the memories you can create. For example, if you already have a perfectly decent TV at home, why buy the newest, more expensive one? Just think of:

- where you could travel to
- what a lovely meal you could have at the fanciest restaurant, or
- how relaxed you will feel after a day at the spa.

Swap your material items for memories and happiness.

Minimalism with Internet

So, you work on the computer, and rather than finishing your report or updating your customer's details, you find yourself browsing through the most obscure information on Wikipedia or Quora, wondering how you ended up there. Or, you are waiting for the bus, and rather than appreciating the drama of the rainclouds or reflections in the puddles, you are aimlessly scrolling down Instagram looking at photos of people you haven't seen in years. Maybe that sounds a little dramatic, but it is so easy to get sucked into the digital world and miss what's going on around us.

Try browsing with intention, and only when you specifically need something. When you are looking for something to do, enjoy the scenery, read a book, or listen to music. This simple act helps you to live more in the moment, and appreciate the little things in life that can be immensely rewarding.

Action Steps

- Start doing one minimalist thing in your day, every day.

- An example could be to limit your online browsing or to take 15 minutes a day to relax and read. It can be making a shopping list for your trip to the supermarket, or saying 'no' to your colleague when they ask you to check something when you're busy with something else. It can also be deciding not to purchase something on a whim and instead saving the money for a trip.

- Keep a note of these small actions that you take towards living a more minimalist life. When you feel you're struggling with Minimalism, or don't think you do enough, take a look at your notes, so you can see all the steps you have taken and what you have accomplished. Make a note about how you felt when you did it, so you can remember any positive feelings you've had from actions towards Minimalism.

PART THREE: HOW TO STAY A MINIMALIST

Chapter Eight: Tips on Sticking to Minimalism

In this chapter, we will look at some tips to sticking to a minimalist life. These will help you if you ever feel you are struggling to keep it up, or are not sure if you are on the right track.

The same way dieting isn't about trying the new fad and expecting a lifelong weight loss (usually it lasts at best a couple of weeks before going back to normal), Minimalism requires reprogramming your mindset. So, rather than thinking about what you don't have, start thinking about how you are now free to focus on your purpose and make your own, deliberate choices that align with what really matters to you.

If you find yourself living like the model minimalist for a couple of weeks before going on a major shopping spree, then this is the chapter for you. Here are some tips to keeping a minimalist lifestyle sustainable.

Focus on Your Values

Always keep your values, your passions, and what you really want at the forefront of your mind. This is your motivation. Also, try rewiring your way of thinking. For example, rather than saying 'I won't go shopping', start thinking 'I want financial freedom and no debt'. Rather than thinking, 'I won't go out this weekend', say, 'I will exercise or spend time with my friends and family'. Try replacing the negative with an affirmative and make your mindset positive.

Take Care of Yourself

When you're feeling down, this is the moment to take time out and focus on your passions and self-care. However, most of us snap into a reckless mentality, such as drinking, to squash down negative feelings or going to the mall for some 'retail therapy'. Try taking good care of yourself, so you feel good and capable of making well-rounded decisions, regardless of the negativity that is in your life at that moment. Make your well-being a priority every day.

Be Mindful

It's very easy to think, *"Well, I'll just buy this new* [insert unnecessary item here] *and then I will have everything I need to be a minimalist."* But how true is that statement really? There is always something else we 'need' to buy or simply 'must' have. It's a cycle and it's one that can be broken by being mindful and appreciating what you already have. Start writing down at least three things per day that you are grateful for. This is a powerful tool to remember what makes you feel genuinely happy, and it is also wonderful to look back on. Prioritize what makes you feel content, and focus on that rather than the material items you feel you need. These little actions can help you stop from always wanting more.

Be Patient

It's likely you are hoping that Minimalism will change something in your life, and it probably can. However, this change won't come overnight. It's important to be patient and recognize this as a journey. You can declutter your entire house, your car, and swear you will never shop again. However, even with these actions, you are still the same person the next day. It will take some time for your mind to reprogram itself.

Don't be Too Hard on Yourself

The minimalist approach can be hard, when surrounded by such a strong consumer culture. Even the smallest of steps should be celebrated. Make sure you look back regularly at your achievements. Reward yourself for it by doing something you love and that nourishes your soul.

Action Steps

- Keep a journal that logs down things that you feel grateful for every day. It doesn't matter what, just write down the things that make you feel happy or thankful. For example, someone giving you a compliment, or watching a beautiful sunrise. Perhaps having your family around you or a great job. You don't need to think of a new list every day; it's fine if you feel thankful for the same thing several days in a row!

- In the same journal, write down the things that you have achieved on your minimalist journey. Reward yourself for accomplishments and learn from the slip ups. It's all part of the journey.

Chapter Nine: What's Next?

So, you started your journey as a minimalist. You have decluttered your house, your car, and your workspace. You haven't had a shopping spree in weeks. You are totally on track. Now what? This chapter will look at the next steps of Minimalism.

Change Your Mindset

Rather than thinking about what you are discarding, focus on what you are keeping and why. This will help you connect with what you want from life in the long-run, rather than what you *don't* want. Remember, Minimalism is less about throwing things out and more about making room for the things you value or find important.

Think About What You Want to Do

Now that you have less material things in your life and have cut those materialistic ties, you are free to do the things you love and are passionate for. Not sure what they are? Then now is your time to experiment and find out. If you love exercising, join different sports groups or start training for a marathon. If art is your thing, join an art class. If you want to give back to society, volunteer. Do things that truly add meaning to your life and start enjoying the best part of Minimalism – doing whatever it is that makes you feel content and happy.

Where Can You Apply Minimalism?

See where else Minimalism can be applied to your life. You may have cut down on material items and freed more time for you and your passions, but how about other areas of your life? Scott Robbins, the husband of one of my good friends, started living more minimally and found it really worked for him as he increasingly found more value, happiness, and time in his life. He decided to see where else he could live minimally and decided to apply it to what he eats. He told me, "*I was living minimally in almost every aspect, but I found I would still buy too much food that would go to waste. I was also buying processed food, which is filled with chemicals. I decided to start only buying natural foods that have few ingredients and I buy local and organic wherever possible. Not only do I feel healthier for this, I also feel I've bonded with my local community. I know exactly where my eggs come from and where my vegetables are grown. Of course, I still buy some foods that could be considered processed but I try and simplify it wherever possible.*"

I recommend you take the same approach.

Action Steps

- Brainstorm all the things you love to do. Start doing at least one of these things per week. You can search online to see if there are local groups in your neighborhood or online. Start filling your time with things you love.

- If you're ready to take the next step, why not see where else you can apply Minimalism, like Scott did? Perhaps making conscious decisions about what food you buy and eat could be a good way to go.

Chapter Ten: The Mindset of a Minimalist (Your Minimalism Blueprint)

Over the last chapters, you have learned what it takes to become a minimalist. In this chapter, you will understand the mindset of one. This will be your blueprint of how a minimalist mind thinks.

So, what is the minimalist mindset?

- It is a mindset that wants less and is content with whatever it already has. A minimalist is grateful for what he has in his life and understands that value in materials is illusory and doesn't provide us true happiness. Instead, our relationships, connections, and passions are the most important things.

- It's one that understands a simple way of living makes an easier and stress-free life.
- It's one that seeks freedom from the consumer culture and only creates physical and mental room for things of value. It makes space for better, more conscious decisions that ultimately lead to a more grounded, fulfilling, and happier life.
- It's one that is free from the ties of unnecessary possessions.
- It's one that can be applied to anyone, it's not a cult or a religion. Minimalism is simply a way of thinking that frees us from materialism and prioritizes what's most important to us.
- It's one that recognizes the impulses in us to consume, and directs them into a passion that is good for our well-being instead. Minimalism is a mindset that makes deliberate choices after careful consideration and focuses on what will bring them value.

Action Steps

- Make a list of all the positive attributes that you want from a minimalist mindset.

- Think about why they are important to you and how they will help you lead a better or happier life if you have a similar mindset.

- Once you have this 'why', the rest – the how, the what and the who – will become more apparent. Knowing why these attributes are important to you will help you find a way to add them to your own way of thinking.

Final Words

Our whole society is based nowadays on striving for bigger and better things. We aren't content unless we have the biggest house on the street, the best car, the most clothes in our huge walk-in wardrobe, the most likes on our Instagram photo, or the most cosmetic treatments.

If this is what makes people truly happy and content, then that's great, I'm all for it. However, the reality is, this lifestyle of always wanting more can be immensely unsatisfying and it never ends. It can also impact negatively on our planet, as the urge to consume more and more gets greater and greater.

In a time where society's focus is on accumulating more and more stuff, it's a relief to be focusing on *less*. That's what Minimalism allows us to do; to let go of the pressures of our culture to consume so much and just focus on what's around us and makes us happy – our loved ones, our professional achievements, our personal development, and our passions.

I hope this book has inspired you to get your feet wet and adopt at least a small amount of Minimalism in your life. You will be on your way to reconnect with what genuinely makes you feel alive. I'm excited for your journey, and I hope you find yourself in a better, happier place.

This book only scratched the surface of what Minimalism is all about. If you would like to continue learning about Minimalism, I suggest you pick up one of the books I recommend in the 'Resources' section.

Best of luck, and enjoy the minimalist way!

Resources

Books on Minimalism

- *The Life-Changing Magic of Tidying Up: The Japanese Art of Decluttering and Organizing* – Marie Kondō
- *Minimalism: Live a Meaningful Life* – Joshua Fields Millburn & Ryan Nicodemus
- *Goodbye, Things: The New Japanese Minimalism* – Fumio Sasaki
- *Essentialism: The Disciplined Pursuit of Less* – Greg McKeown
- *Declutter Your Life: The Art of Tidying Up, Organizing Your Home, Decluttering Your Mind, and Minimalist Living (Less is More!)* – Kevin Garnett

Websites on Minimalism

- Theminimalists.com
- Becomingminimalist.com
- Bemorewithless.com
- Minimalism.life
- NewMinimalism.com
- Theartofsimple.net
- Reddit.com/r/Minimalism/

Documentaries on Minimalism

- Minimalism: a Documentary about the Important Things
- TINY: A Story About Living Small
- My Stuff (Tavarataivas)

YouTube Channels on Minimalism

- The Minimalists

- Jenny Mustard
- Matt D'Avella
- Lavendaire

Podcasts on Minimalism

- The Minimalists
- The Simple Show
- The Slow Home
- 10% Happier
- Zen Commuter
- Optimal Living Daily

BONUS CHAPTER: What is Stoicism

Below, you will find a free bonus chapter from my book **'STOICISM FOR BEGINNERS**: Master the Art of Happiness. Learn Modern, Practical Stoicism to Create Your Own Daily Stoic Routine.'

Enjoy!

It is my way of saying thanks for

- *Reading this book, and*
- *Taking your first step on the path of Minimalism. You rock!*

Let's get started, shall we?

***

In this chapter, you are going to learn what Stoicism is and where it originates.

In recent years, interest in the ancient philosophy of Stoicism has experienced a renaissance. Despite the growing popularity of this older philosophy, there are still so many misconceptions about it. For instance, many people believe that Stoicism is about being devoid of any emotion, including happiness. Others think that to be a stoic, you need to lead a Spartan and bland lifestyle. To set the records straight, let's take a look at what Stoicism really is.

What is Stoicism?

Stoicism is a philosophy that helps us maintain control over our thoughts and actions in a world full of chaos and unpredictability. Stoicism understands that we have no control over external occurrences, and therefore we should not rely on them. Instead, we should rely on our mind, behavior, and reaction to external events, all of which we can control. Stoicism teaches us that what matters is not what *happens* to us, but rather, how we *react* to it. In a world of chaos, Stoicism teaches us how to remain steadfast, strong and in control of ourselves.

Most of our dissatisfaction in life occurs because, rather than using logic, we have an impulsive dependency on our reflexes. Stoicism helps us to:

- overcome these destructive emotions,
- act on what we can act upon, and
- accept things that we cannot act upon.

Rather than being a philosophy of endless debate, Stoicism is **focused on action**.

The core principle of this ancient philosophy is that we need to overcome our insatiability in order for us to lead good and meaningful lives. Most people today live their lives like slaves, always in pursuit of happiness. Every person has a long list of desires that they are trying to satisfy. Even those you consider to have attained success have more things they want to achieve. The problem is that, once one desire is satisfied, it tends to be immediately replaced by a new one. This keeps most of us in continuous chase, always trying to satisfy our desires. After a lifetime of pursuit, we are no more satisfied than we were at the very start. This way, we end up wasting our lives instead of living for each moment.

Stoicism is a philosophy that should be applied in our day to day lives. It focuses on ethics (how we live our lives), which are in turn influenced by the natural world and logic. The resurgence of the popularity of Stoicism in the modern world has been driven by the fact that the philosophy aims to teach us how to attain peace, joy and tranquility in the midst of struggles and hardship.

The Origin of Stoicism

Stoicism was founded in Athens in the early 3rd century BC. The philosophy was founded by a

Phoenician merchant and philosopher known as Zeno. Zeno was born in Citium, a town in Cyprus, and lived from 334 to 262 BC. At around the age of 34, during one of his travels, Zeno was shipwrecked. Luckily, he survived and found himself in Athens. Having lost everything and with nothing else to do in life, he visited a bookseller in Athens. It is here that he found a book that would lead him on the path of becoming a philosopher. After learning under Crates of Thebes and the philosophers of the Megarian School, he then began teaching and practicing his own philosophy. His school of philosophy was known as Zenoism, before the name was later changed to Stoicism. The name Stoicism was derived from the Stoa Poikile, a 'painted porch' from where Zeno used to give his lectures. His students became known as 'Stoics'.

Stoicism was not a philosophy that was reserved for the aristocrats. It was a philosophy of the street, open for ordinary people. A *working class* philosophy, if you will! Anyone could go to the Stoa Poikile and listen to the teachings of Zeno.

The philosophy taught and practiced by Zeno as well as other Stoic philosophers was heavily influenced by the works of Socrates. Apart from Socrates, Stoicism was also influenced by the Cynics, the Skeptics and the Academics (the followers of Plato).

While Stoicism was founded by Zeno, one of the most influential Greek Stoics was Chrysippus, who was one of Zeno's followers. Chrysippus is said to have elaborated most of the doctrines that are associated with the philosophy to this day. Apart from Plato, Socrates and Aristotle, Chrysippus is believed to be the greatest ancient philosopher. Though he is believed to have authored over 700 works, unfortunately none of them survived.

Despite having originated in ancient Greece, the greatest influence of Stoicism would be felt centuries later when it got to the Roman Empire. Most of what is known about Stoicism today comes from the ideas and writings of the Roman Stoics. Some of the most influential Stoics from this era include Epictetus, Musonius Rufus, Seneca and Marcus Aurelius.

Owing to the kind of lives led by the early Stoic philosophers, Stoicism was perceived as a very practical and very useful school of thought from its early stages. It later moved from Athens to the West, where it gained lots of popularity. However, the adoption of Christianity as the official Roman religion and its subsequent spread to the west led to the decline of Stoicism and several other ancient Greek philosophies. People abandoned this ancient philosophy to the point where it almost became extinct.

Fortunately, Stoic Philosophy started making a comeback in the late 20th Century. This resurgence has been driven by a number of factors. These include the adoption of the philosophy by celebrities and pop culture idols, featuring of the philosophy in the works of renowned authors as well as the growing interest in self-development. Some popular business and political leaders who have been known to practice Stoicism include Bill Gates, Warren Buffet, Tim Ferris, Tony Robbins, Presidents George Washington and Theodore Roosevelt, as well as actor/musician LL Cool J.

In the next chapter, you are going to learn the key beliefs and principles beliefs of Stoicism.

The Most Important Stoic Philosophers

In the next chapter, you are going to learn the beliefs and principles that form the foundation of the philosophy of Stoicism.

They are based on the teachings of three Stoic leaders:

- **Marcus Aurelius**: Aurelius was an Emperor of the Roman Empire, and the last one among the five so-called good Emperors. Perhaps you remember him from the first scenes of the 2000 movie *Gladiator*. During this time, Aurelius was the most powerful person on earth. He had everything under his command, he could fulfill any of his desires, yet he exercised great restraint against his temptations. Each evening, Marcus Aurelius sat down alone, reflected on his day and wrote his thoughts in a private diary. His diary was later published as the book *Meditations*. This book has been one of the most significant sources of knowledge about Stoic philosophy.

- **Epictetus**: Despite the fame he had attained by the time of his death, Epictetus was born as a slave. Epictetus discovered Stoicism through another Stoic philosopher known as Musonius Rufus. When he gained his freedom, Epictetus founded his own school and went ahead to teach many great people in Rome, one of whom was Marcus Aurelius. Epictetus never wrote down his teachings. His influence came by pure luck through one of his students – Arrian – who wrote down his teachings. Arrian wrote two books, Discourses and Enchiridion, which contain most of the teachings of Epictetus.

- **Seneca**: Seneca was a renowned playwright, an advisor to emperor Nero, and one of the wealthiest people within the Roman Empire. Seneca was exposed to Stoicism by Attalus, a Stoic philosopher who tutored him in his early life. He was also a great admirer of Cato. Many of Seneca's personal letters and writings survived after his death and have been a great source of knowledge on Stoicism. Seneca's writings had great influence on some notable people, including Erasmus, Pascal, Francis Bacon and Montaigne.

With that out of the way, let's dive into the most important beliefs and principles of Stoic philosophy.

***

This is the end of this bonus chapter. Want to continue reading? Then get your copy of "Stoicism for Beginners" at your favorite bookstore!

Did You Like This Book?

If you enjoyed this book, I would like to ask you for a favor. Would you be kind enough to share your thoughts and post a review of this book? Just a few sentences would already be really helpful.

Your voice is important for this book to reach as many people as possible.

The more reviews this book gets, the more people will be able to find it and learn how Minimalism can change their lives!

***

IF YOU DID NOT LIKE THIS BOOK, THEN PLEASE TELL ME! You can email me at **feedback@semsoli.com**, to share with me what you did not like.

Perhaps I can change it.

A book does not have to be stagnant, in today's world. With feedback from readers like yourself, I can improve the book. So you can impact the quality of this book, and I welcome your feedback. Help make this book better for everyone!

Thank you again for reading this book and good luck with applying everything you have learned!

I'm rooting for you...

By The Same Author

Notes